EXTREME SURVIVAL

HOW PEOPLE, PLANTS, AND ANIMALS LIVE IN THE WORLD'S TOUGHEST PLACES

For the Rose boys—Sam, Ben, and Patrick—wherever they may roam. B. L.

For Hannah and Hendrix the dog for keeping me sane this year. D. L.

First published in 2022 by Nosy Crow Ltd.
Wheat Wharf, 27a Shad Thames,
London, SE1 2XZ, UK

This edition published 2024 by Nosy Crow Inc.
145 Lincoln Road, Lincoln, MA 01773, USA

www.nosycrow.com

ISBN 979-8-88777-048-2

Nosy Crow and associated logos are trademarks of Nosy Crow Ltd.
Used under license.

Text © Ben Lerwill 2022
Illustrations © Daniel Long 2022

Library of Congress Catalog Card Number pending.

Printed in China.
Papers used by Nosy Crow are made from wood
grown in sustainable forests.

1 3 5 7 9 8 6 4 2

EXTREME SURVIVAL

HOW PEOPLE, PLANTS, AND ANIMALS LIVE IN THE WORLD'S TOUGHEST PLACES

written by
BEN LERWILL

illustrated by
DANIEL LONG

CONTENTS

INTRODUCTION

Have you ever dreamed of exploring distant lands? Of hiking through the sweltering depths of the Amazon Rainforest, or crossing the freezing plains of the Arctic? Going on a big adventure is always exciting—but it's even better when you're well prepared.

That's what this book is for. Over the following pages, we'll be traveling all the way around the world, visiting all kinds of incredible places, and learning tricks and tips for staying safe. What happens if you get caught in a desert sandstorm? How do you build an igloo? And what's the best way to escape a shark?

Humans need four basic things to survive: food, water, warmth, and shelter. But when you're on an expedition, survival is often about much more than that. It's about understanding your environment and knowing how to stay healthy and well. It's about looking after the people you're with and the place you're visiting.

And above all, it's about being able to enjoy the adventure!

ARCTIC CIRCLE

Picture a world of snow, ice, and bone-chillingly cold water. A place where you can hear your breath crackling as it freezes in the air. This is the long Arctic winter, when the sun rarely rises above the horizon and the skies can stay dark for weeks, or even months. Life is hard up here in the far north: the distances are huge, the cold is extreme, and the nights are long. Months from now, when summer arrives, this will be a very different place. Until then, white hills and frozen lakes sit under silent skies. The polar landscape sometimes looks lifeless, but among the icy bays and islands, nature finds a way to survive . . .

FACT FILE

» The Arctic Circle is the name given to the area north of an imaginary line measuring 10,000 miles around the top of the world.

» Parts of Russia, Canada, Greenland, Alaska, and Scandinavia are all within the Arctic Circle.

» Most of the Arctic Circle is ocean. Some parts of it stay frozen as sea ice all year.

» Along with Antarctica in the far south, the Arctic Circle is one of Earth's two polar regions.

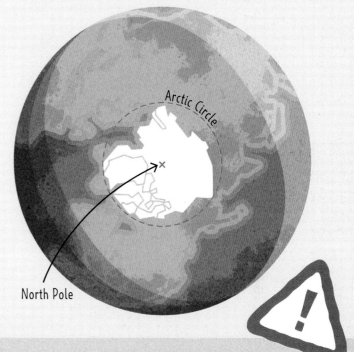

Arctic Circle

North Pole

THINGS TO **REMEMBER**

Temperatures can fall below -58 °F, so staying warm will save your life.

Staying dry is vital too. If you get wet, you'll lose heat dangerously quickly.

Wild winds can make the air feel even colder.

If you're walking over ice, always make sure it's strong enough to support you.

WHO **LIVES** HERE?

The Arctic Circle covers an enormous area. Most of it is wilderness, but these days there are also villages, towns, and even cities. Experts think people have been living in this part of the world for as long as 20,000 years. Peoples such as the Inuit, from Greenland and Canada, and the Yupik, from Alaska and Russia, have had to learn the best ways to survive the long Arctic winters. Some still live in remote areas and practice traditional ways of hunting and fishing, though modern technology has made survival easier. Adventurers from around the world also come to the Arctic Circle.

Sealskin is naturally waterproof. Some people who live here still use it to make gloves and shoes.

WHAT ELSE **SURVIVES** HERE?

Some of the planet's most incredible creatures have evolved to live in the Arctic Circle—above and below the sea ice!

Polar bears have white shaggy fur to blend in with their surroundings.

Narwhals use their long tusks to stun and catch cold-water fish.

Arctic foxes have bushy tails that they can wrap around themselves to stay warm.

WHAT ARE . . .
THE NORTHERN LIGHTS?

On dark, clear nights, magic fills the Arctic sky. Rainbow-colored shapes shimmer across the heavens, gliding and glowing. The northern lights are one of nature's most amazing displays . . . but what are they?

The lights are caused by solar particles, which are tiny specks of matter sent out by the sun. When these particles get close to Earth, they're attracted to the polar regions, which are magnetic. Here, they collide with gases in the atmosphere, making the sky glow with light.

The lights are mostly green or pink, but can also be yellow, orange, violet, or blue.

THE STORY OF...
ADA BLACKJACK

Wrangel is an ice-cold Russian island roamed by polar bears. It's not the kind of place you'd choose to be stuck for two years—but this is exactly what happened to a brave young Iñupiaq woman named Ada Blackjack, from Alaska. She was just 23 years old when she arrived here in 1921 as a helper on an expedition, but the other members of the team soon died, leaving just Ada and a cat named Victoria to survive alone. She set traps to catch foxes, learned how to shoot birds, and even made a small boat from animal skins. When a rescue ship finally arrived two years later, the crew found both Ada and Victoria alive. Back home in Alaska, Ada found work as a reindeer herder and lived to the age of 85.

HOW TO...
BUILD AN IGLOO

These traditional snow-domes are still used as temporary winter shelters by some Inuit. They can be surprisingly cozy!

Most of the Arctic Circle has no trees . . . which means no firewood. In the past, people lit lamps filled with seal fat or lichen (a mossy plant) to make small fires.

1 First, dig down past the powdery surface snow until you reach hard compact snow. Using a snow saw, cut this hard snow into thick rectangular blocks.

2 Start arranging the blocks into a circular wall. The top of the wall should slope gradually upward. The space inside should be big enough for you to lie down comfortably.

3 Keep building the igloo, block by block, in a spiral pattern, until you've made a dome shape. Make sure you leave space for a small hole at the top. This helps the air circulate.

4 Cut a low doorway that you can crawl into. To keep more warmth in, you can even tunnel under the wall to make an underground doorway!

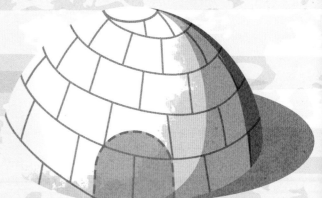

5 It's dangerous to sleep directly on snow or ice, so cover the ground inside the igloo with whatever you have. Inuit traditionally used birch twigs and animal furs.

NORTH POLE EXPLORERS

At the very top of the world map—in the exact middle of the Arctic Circle—you'll find the North Pole. It's not actually on land at all, but on a thick shelf of sea ice. This makes it very difficult to reach. Even today, no one's quite sure who the first explorer was to arrive here!

Some people say it was an American named Frederick Cook and his two Inuit guides, Ahwelah and Etukishook. Cook claimed they had reached the pole in 1908, after a difficult expedition that lasted months. Other people say it was another American, Robert E. Peary, who battled his way to the North Pole in 1909. We may never know the truth!

Ahwelah, Etukishook,
and Frederick Cook

Robert E. Peary

Robert E. Peary

Ahwelah, Etukishook,
and Frederick Cook

When they wanted to travel long distances, some Inuit used to make sleds by stretching animal skin over whale bones. The sleds were then pulled across the ice by dogs.

WHAT IS...
ICE FISHING?

Ice fishing is a way of catching fish when the sea, or a lake, is frozen. It's done by drilling a hole into the ice and dangling a rod and line into the water below. The hole should be big enough to pull a fish through but not large enough to slip into.

The glare from ice and snow can be blinding. If you don't have snow goggles, cut small slits into pieces of wood or cardboard and place them over your eyes.

The crucial thing to remember is that the ice needs to be strong enough to support whoever's on it. Imagine a toilet paper roll standing on its end—if the ice isn't at least as thick as this, it's far too dangerous to stand on!

THE CHANGING ARCTIC

The summer months bring big changes to the Arctic Circle, with warmth, greenery, and sunlight. On some days the sun never sets at all—even at midnight! These higher temperatures melt away lots of the ice and snow, although large areas stay frozen all year because the ice is so thick.

This is good for animals like polar bears, and good for the world as a whole, because the ice here reflects sunlight, which keeps the planet cooler.

But there's a problem. Global warming means too much ice is melting. This not only damages the Arctic environment, it also makes the planet even warmer.

WAYS TO HELP THE ARCTIC CIRCLE

REDUCE YOUR CARBON FOOTPRINT

The Arctic Circle is warming up faster than anywhere else in the world. By cutting our carbon emissions, we can slow this down.

GIVE GREEN ENERGY THE THUMBS UP

Check which company supplies your gas and electricity at home. You could ask the person who pays the bill to switch to a green energy supplier.

JOIN THE TEAM

Get involved with amazing organizations like Polar Bears International, which helps protect polar bears.

NORTH AMERICAN
FORESTS

Dry twigs crunch underfoot. Birdsong echoes among tall pine trees. You're in the forests of North America, where rivers thunder through wild backwoods and the nearest road is a full day's walk away. Trout splash in the water, hawks soar overhead, and half-seen mammals disappear behind trees. The forest seems to go on for ever, rolling over hills and stretching through valleys—but if you know how to look after yourself, it's an amazing place to be.

FACT FILE

» Large forests like this are found across Canada as well as in US states like Alaska, Washington, and Idaho. They cover large parts of northern Europe and Asia too.

» They're also known as "boreal forests"—named after Boreas, the Greek god of the north wind.

» Most of the trees here are coniferous, which means they keep their leaves year-round. The main species are larch, spruce, and pine.

THINGS TO REMEMBER

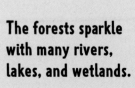

Large animals such as bears and moose are found here.

Getting lost is easy if you don't have a map or a plan.

The forests sparkle with many rivers, lakes, and wetlands.

Paths can often become soggy and flooded.

WHO **LIVES** HERE?

The Indigenous peoples of the US and Canada settled in the plains and forests of this region thousands of years ago. Traditionally, they survived by hunting, trapping, and fishing, often using spears and bows and arrows. They moved around in search of food, and were skilled at making homes from wooden poles and animal skins, called tipis. They also made canoes from natural materials such as birch tree bark.

Over 500 years ago, non-Indigenous people began arriving from other countries. They stole land from the Indigenous peoples and treated them in ways that were very unfair. Today, many people from different backgrounds still live and work in remote and rural communities here.

WHAT ELSE **SURVIVES** HERE?

The boreal forests of North America have short summers and long winters, and the animals that live here have adapted to survive in the harsh, cold habitat.

Wood bison have thick wooly coats to keep them warm.

Black-backed woodpeckers have long tongues to reach insect larvae hiding under tree bark.

Porcupines have thousands of sharp quills to keep hungry predators away.

TIPS FOR **MAKING A FIRE**

Remember: NEVER make a fire unless you have a grown-up to help you!

- First, clear the area where you want to make the fire, removing any leaves or branches.
- Gather dry grass, small twigs, and larger twigs.
- Start small. Make a "nest" of dry grass and small twigs. Some people put cotton balls covered in petroleum jelly (such as Vaseline) in the nest, because it lights easily.
- Make sure no hair or clothing will be dangling over the fire. Have a big container of water close by in case of emergencies.
- To light the fire, kneel with the wind at your back. This shelters the fire and lets smoke drift away from you. If you're using matches, always strike them AWAY from your body.
- When you have a small nest-fire, arrange the larger twigs in a pyramid around it.
- When the fire is burning well, you can begin carefully adding larger, thicker pieces of wood. Try to keep the pyramid shape.
- A lit fire must ALWAYS be watched by someone.
- To put a fire out, let the flames die down then use a long stick to spread out the pieces of wood. Gently pour water on the embers. Always make sure the fire is completely out before you leave it.

Stay on marked trails. They stop you from getting lost and also help to protect the forest.

BEWARE OF **THE BEARS!**

Grizzly bears and black bears are both found in North American forests. They try to stay away from humans, but they can be aggressive if they're taken by surprise.

- If you're walking through bear country, be noisy! If a bear hears you singing, talking, or clapping, it will know you're coming and move away.
- If you're camping, never keep food, trash, or cooking equipment in your tent. Even the smell of toothpaste can attract bears. Keep everything well away from your tent, in strong, tightly sealed containers.
- If you do come face to face with a bear, stay still and talk calmly, so that it knows you're a human. Wave your arms slowly above your head to look bigger. Never stand between a mother and her cubs.

Try not to hike before breakfast or after dinner, when wildlife is most likely to be on the move.

HOW TO...
LOOK AFTER A CUT

If you get a cut or scrape, stay calm and remember the three key things you need to do.

1 Stop the bleeding. You can usually do this by pressing a clean towel or handkerchief against the cut.

2 Wash the cut with drinking water, to make sure it's clean.

3 Pat it dry and cover with a Band-Aid or dressing.

? **WAYS TO HELP** FORESTS

NEVER LEAVE LITTER

Even small scraps of trash can be harmful to forest wildlife, so always take your litter with you.

PROTEST AGAINST LOGGING

When large areas of forest are cut down by loggers, it can take centuries for the forest to return to how it used to be.

PROTECT THE PLANTS

Don't cut, chop, or damage any forest trees or wild plants unless you absolutely need to.

THE OCEAN

Turtles swimming over colorful reefs. Whales ghosting through the blue. Trenches and sea caves, currents and corals, sharks and shipwrecks. The ocean is a universe of its own, a watery infinity so big, deep, and wide that experts think it could be home to more than a million different species. In fact, it's so large that it covers more than 70% of the planet's surface! Divers, sailors, scientists, adventurers, and submariners all explore the ocean—but whether you're above the waves or below them, you need to think clearly to stay safe.

FACT FILE

» Around 97% of all water on Earth is found in the sea.

» Have you ever heard people talk about the seven seas? It's a way of describing the world's seven main ocean areas: the Arctic Ocean, the Antarctic (or Southern) Ocean, the South Atlantic, the North Atlantic, the South Pacific, the North Pacific, and the Indian Ocean.

» The deepest part of the ocean is the Mariana Trench in the North Pacific. Its lowest point is almost 7 miles below the waves. That's deeper than Mount Everest is tall!

THINGS TO REMEMBER

There might be water everywhere you look, but it's not drinkable. Drinking salty seawater just makes you thirstier!

Sunburn can be just as big a problem at sea as it is on land.

When seawater is moving continuously in one direction, we call it a sea current. These currents can be very strong and very dangerous.

If you're lost at sea, staying calm will save your energy—and maybe save your life too.

WHO **SPENDS TIME** HERE?

The world's oceans are constantly busy with fishing vessels, passenger ferries, cargo ships, and other boats. Some people live and work on oil rigs, which are drilling platforms out at sea. Beneath the waves, submarines and submersibles navigate the depths. Submersibles are small underwater craft typically used for science or exploration. Submarines are enclosed boats that can travel deep underwater. They can have crews of up to 150 people, and can stay below the surface for several months at a time!

WHAT ELSE **SURVIVES** HERE?

The ocean is home to an enormous variety of fish and other sea creatures, ranging from tiny plankton to enormous whales.

Giant squid have huge eyes to help them see in the deepest, darkest oceans.

Bottlenose dolphins use their powerful tails to swim fast and leap into the air.

Parrotfish have strong "beaks" to chew algae from coral reefs.

WHAT IS **SCUBA DIVING**?

Have you ever wanted to explore the seabed, or swim surrounded by tropical fish? Scuba diving lets you swim underwater with a tank of air on your back. When divers swim really deep, they have to be careful to go down and come back up slowly. If they do this too fast, the changing water pressure can be dangerous to the human body. Scuba stands for "self-contained underwater breathing apparatus"—in other words, something that helps you breathe when you're below the waves!

If you start feeling seasick on a boat, stand near the front of the boat and keep your eyes on the horizon ahead. This usually helps you feel better.

WHAT TO DO IF ... **YOU SEE A SHARK**

There are hundreds of different shark species in the sea, and only a tiny number of them are dangerous to humans. If you do spot a large fin when you're in the water, the best thing to do is to swim quickly and calmly to a safe place. Sharks sometimes attack humans because they think we're seals or sea lions, which are their natural prey. If you see a fin zigzagging toward you—which is very unlikely!—shout for help. If you're in real danger, try to bump the shark as hard as possible in the eyes, nose, or gills. These are the softest, most sensitive parts of a shark's body, and it should back off.

If your boat gets lost at sea, rainwater is your best chance of finding something to drink. Catch it by using a tarp, plastic bag, or anything else you can find.

If you're stranded in cold water, there's a real danger of your body losing too much heat. If you have a life vest on, get into the Heat Escape Lessening Position, or HELP, which will help you stay warmer. Do this by folding your arms across your chest, crossing your feet, and pulling your knees up.

WAYS TO HELP THE OCEAN

DON'T THROW THINGS OVERBOARD

If you're traveling by boat, don't throw anything overboard. One plastic bottle can take 450 years to decompose.

PROTECT CORAL REEFS

Corals can be harmed by global warming. And although they might look like plants or rocks, they're actually animals, so never touch or tread on them.

WEAR THE RIGHT SUNSCREEN

It's very important to wear sunscreen, but some lotions contain chemicals that harm marine life. Choose a sunscreen lotion without chemicals.

AMAZON
RAINFOREST

The heat of the jungle is all around you. You hear the drone of insects, the hoots of monkeys, the squawks of colorful birds. Your nose is filled with the thick scents of tropical plants. The air is so hot and humid that your clothes are damp and your hair sticks to your forehead. Lines of ants crawl over the forest floor, mosquitoes buzz around your head and, no matter which way you turn, you face a tangle of branches and creepers. The Amazon Rainforest is a magical, beautiful place—but you need to stay alert to stay safe.

FACT FILE

» It's the largest tropical rainforest on the planet, covering more than 2.5 million square miles. That's more than half the size of the US!

» Most of the rainforest is in Brazil, but it also stretches into eight other South American countries.

» The Amazon River, one of the world's longest rivers, runs through the rainforest.

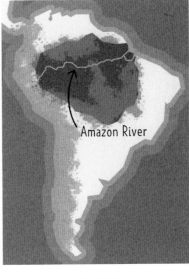

Amazon River

THINGS TO REMEMBER

 Moving through the jungle can be very difficult and tiring.

 Some of the plants are poisonous—and so are some of the animals!

 It's easy to get lost among the trees and hills.

 It's a rainforest—so when it rains, it really rains!

WHO **LIVES** HERE?

People have lived in settlements in the Amazon Rainforest for thousands of years. They understand how to live in the jungle much better than most outsiders. They know which plants can help them, and which animals and insects to stay away from. Even today, around 400 groups of Indigenous peoples live in the Amazon. Many now have modern ways of life and live close to the river, where they can travel by boat, but some still live deep in the jungle, far from any towns or cities. Some have never had any contact with the outside world at all.

RAINFOREST **FOOD**

All kinds of delicious things grow in the Amazon Rainforest: papayas, pineapples, mangoes, and countless other wild fruits, nuts, and plants, including acai berries, small purple fruit that grow on tall palm trees.

It's vital to be sure that any plant you eat is safe. The last thing you need in a remote rainforest is to get sick from eating something poisonous, because finding help can be almost impossible. So if you don't recognize it, don't eat it—even if you're really hungry!

In an emergency situation, healthy humans can only last a few days without water, but they can survive much longer without eating!

WHAT ELSE **SURVIVES** HERE?

Life is everywhere in the Amazon Rainforest. It has hundreds of reptile and mammal species, thousands of different birds and fish, and more than two million types of insect!

Scarlet macaws have large, strong beaks to crack nuts and eat fruit and berries.

Spider monkeys have four long limbs (and a tail they can grip with!) to climb trees.

Giant anteaters have claws to dig up ants and termites—and long sticky tongues to eat them with!

THE AMAZING STORY OF
JULIANE KOEPCKE

In 1971, a plane flying over the Amazon Rainforest crashed into the jungle. The only person who survived was a 17-year-old girl named Juliane Koepcke. She was cut and bruised but alive, and found herself alone in the middle of the thick, sweltering rainforest. It was a frightening situation, but she stayed calm.

Juliane knew that to survive, she needed to find people to help her. She found a jungle stream, which she followed downhill until it became a river, remembering that people often live near water. Finally, after 10 exhausting days, she spotted an empty boat. She stayed close to it, and soon some local fishermen found her and came to the rescue. Her incredible adventure was over.

HOW TO... FIND WATER

Water is probably the most important thing you need to survive in the jungle, but you can't just find a stream and start drinking. If you don't know what's in the water, it could easily make you sick.

Be careful when moving rocks or branches. You might disturb spiders or other creatures living underneath.

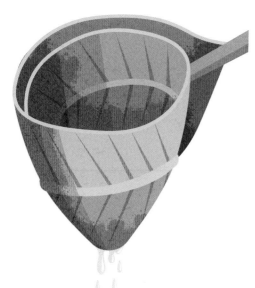

It rains a lot in the Amazon, so try collecting clean rainwater, using a big leaf as a funnel.

A lot of plants hold water in their stems. Bamboo is very good for this. Give a stick of bamboo a shake. If you can hear water inside, make a hole at the bottom of each bamboo section and collect the water as it comes out. It's usually very fresh, but don't drink it if it smells bad!

If you can, you should always boil water over a fire (see page 16) or use water purification tablets, which kill germs and make water safer to drink.

WHAT IS... A BLOWPIPE?

Some Indigenous peoples of the Amazon have traditionally used spears, arrows, and blowpipes to hunt food like fish or turtles. A blowpipe is a hollow tube that can be used to blow out darts.

By aiming the blowpipe then blowing hard into the tube, they shoot the darts through the air.

The tube is made by hollowing out a straight branch, using a pointed bone or stick.

The darts are small, sharp pieces of palm leaf.

Some Indigenous peoples dip their darts in poison, which they get from poisonous plants, or from the poisonous skin of a specific type of frog! Because of this, it's known as the poison dart frog.

HOW TO . . .
BUILD A SHELTER

First, find a high area of land, so you won't be flooded in the night.

Gather some strong, straight branches, using vines as string to tie them together in a tent shape. Make them as sturdy as possible.

If you want to stay camouflaged, avoid wearing bright colors. And remember—many Amazon animals know how to stay hidden too!

Use thick leaves, long grasses, and palm fronds to make a roof. The better the roof, the more waterproof the shelter.

Don't sleep directly on the forest floor, where there are lots of insects. Survival experts often use branches to make a raised bed, then cover it in palm fronds and fern leaves to make it softer.

? WAYS TO HELP RAINFORESTS

AVOID PALM OIL

In some parts of the world, precious rainforests are being destroyed to make space for palm oil plantations.

EAT LESS BEEF

Deforestation is a serious problem in the Amazon. Huge areas are being chopped down to create land for cattle farmers.

OTHER RAINFORESTS

The Amazon might be our biggest rainforest, but there are many others around the world. In fact, rainforest covers more than a tenth of land on Earth!

In the rainforests of Borneo and Sumatra in Asia, orangutans build treetop nests. Because parts of the jungle are being cut down, they're in danger of losing their homes.

In Costa Rica in Central America, some of the jungles are so high and misty that they're known as cloud forests. They're home to brightly feathered birds like quetzals.

In the thick Congo Rainforest in Africa, the wildlife includes forest elephants, chimpanzees, and even gorillas, the biggest apes in the world.

DESERT ISLAND

You're alone on an empty beach, somewhere in the wide blue
Pacific Ocean. The sun shines down on soft white sand and tall
palm trees. Waves wash against the shore, tropical fruit clusters
in the branches, and exotic birds twitter overhead. It sounds
like the perfect vacation spot—but this is no vacation. Being
stranded on a desert island calls for clever survival techniques
and plenty of patience and courage. You might be rescued in
a day, a month, or a decade . . . and it's up to you to stay calm.

FACT FILE

» The Pacific Ocean is the biggest and
deepest ocean on Earth, and has an
estimated 25,000 islands.

» Some of these islands are large and
inhabited, but the vast majority are
empty of human life.

» The word "desert" in "desert island"
comes from "deserted." It describes a
remote island where no people live.
A desert island isn't actually a desert!

THINGS TO **REMEMBER**

It's not always sunny on Pacific islands. Hurricanes and tropical storms can be fierce, frightening, and soaking wet!

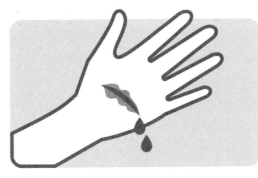

Cuts can become infected, so try hard to keep any wounds clean.

Finding fresh water and somewhere to shelter should be the two things you think about first.

WHO **LIVES** HERE?

Some Pacific islands are home to tens of thousands of people—but true desert islands are different. It would be very unusual for anyone to choose to live on one. If you did end up here, it would typically be because of a shipwreck or a plane crash. However, by understanding how people on Pacific islands have traditionally lived, you can improve your own chance of survival. On many islands, for example, people still catch fish and seafood from the sea, and live in the most sheltered bays to protect themselves from winds and storms.

WHAT ELSE **SURVIVES** HERE?

Staying alive on a desert island can be a serious challenge for humans, but many birds and animals feel at home here.

Sea turtles swim around coral reefs, feeding on shrimps, sponges, jellyfish, or seagrass, and use island beaches to nest and lay their eggs.

White-tailed tropicbirds fly over the sea looking for fish and squid to catch.

Fruit bats roost in high trees and eat fruit and nectar from island plants.

HOW TO... **GET RESCUED**

If you're all alone on a desert island, you should do everything possible to be seen by passing ships or planes. There are a few things you can try.

- Build a fire, sending smoke into the air. If you throw a few wet leaves on to the flames, the fire will get even smokier.
- Use branches, leaves, or rocks to spell out "SOS" or "HELP" on the beach in very big letters.
- If you have a watch, a pocket mirror, or anything else with a shiny surface, use this to reflect sunlight in the direction of the ship or plane.
- Use a branch and a colorful piece of clothing to make a flag, then stand on high ground and wave it.

If you've survived a shipwreck, look for things in the wreckage that might help you. Food, rubber boots (to stop your feet from getting cut), and a good knife could all be very valuable.

THE LONE WOMAN OF
SAN NICOLAS ISLAND

Life on a desert island can be hard, but one amazing woman lived alone on an island in the North Pacific—for 18 years! Today we remember her as the "Lone Woman of San Nicolas Island." She was the last member of her people, the Nicoleño, and from 1835 until 1853 she survived here completely alone. When sailors came to the island, they discovered she had made a hut from whale bones and branches. She spoke a language that no one living could understand, so we'll never know what her real name was or exactly how she stayed alive, but historians think she hunted ducks and seals from the sea, and used bird feathers and animal skins to make clothes.

HOW TO... FIND WATER AND FOOD

You can't drink seawater, so it's essential to find fresh water as soon as you can. Look for streams or small rivers, and leave out containers to collect rainwater. You might also find fresh water dripping from the roofs of some caves.

Another idea is to tie rags round your ankles and walk through long grass before sunrise. The rags will collect the morning dew, which you can then squeeze out.

For food, look for fruit you recognize, like coconuts or wild bananas. If you're patient when trying to catch something, the sea holds plenty of food too. Fish, mussels, and even some seaweed can be eaten. Always cook seafood on a fire before tasting it.

Watch out for falling coconuts—they're very heavy. Some people say falling coconuts kill more people each year than sharks do!

⚠️ WAYS TO HELP DESERT ISLANDS

FIGHT CLIMATE CHANGE
Melting glaciers are leading to rising sea levels, which means some Pacific islands might disappear completely.

TRY NOT TO USE ANY DISPOSABLE PLASTIC ITEMS
A lot of plastic ends up in the ocean, where it badly affects marine life and often clusters around small islands.

KEEP BEACHES CLEAN
Always pick up any litter that's been dropped or washed ashore.

THE ALPS

It's summer in the European Alps. Fluffy white clouds hang in the sky above the peaks and valleys. The sunny slopes are covered in forests, meadows, and hiking paths. Cows graze, their bells clanking softly, and lakes sparkle in the distance. It's the perfect place for an outdoor adventure, whether you're walking, climbing, cycling, or camping. But although it looks peaceful, it's also somewhere you need to take care. Staying safe is the best way to enjoy spending time in this spectacular part of the world.

THINGS TO REMEMBER

 Mountain weather can change quickly, so make sure you're prepared for all conditions.

 Stick to marked trails where possible and always let people know where you're going.

FACT FILE

» The Alps are Europe's largest mountain range, measuring about 620 miles from west to east.

» The mountain range stretches across eight different countries: France, Switzerland, Monaco, Liechtenstein, Italy, Austria, Germany, and Slovenia.

» Its highest peak is Mont Blanc on the border between France and Italy. It's 15,780 feet high—but its exact height depends on how much snow has fallen!

The peak of Mont Blanc

WHO **LIVES** HERE?

Look down into the valleys and you'll see they are dotted with towns and villages. Snow covers the Alps in the colder months, so many of these villages become ski resorts during the winter. However, further up the slopes, there are small mountain huts and farms. Some of these have been used for centuries by farmers, who keep their cattle or goats in the valleys during the snowy season, then lead them up the mountains to graze in high meadows during the summer. Traditionally, these people survived by making cheese from cows' milk, and growing vegetables in the high meadows.

WHAT ELSE **SURVIVES** HERE?

The animals of the Alps have to adapt to warm summers and cold winters—but the mountains give them plenty of shelter and food.

Alpine ibexes have hooves split into two toes, to help them climb steep slopes.

Alpine choughs use caves or mountain crevices for their nests.

Alpine marmots hibernate for more than half the year, to protect themselves from the cold.

HOW TO... **ESTIMATE THE LENGTH OF A WALK**

Guessing how long it's going to take to hike from one place to another can be tricky, especially in the mountains. But by using something called Naismith's Rule, you can work out an approximate time for your journey.

First, use a map to measure how far you're going to walk, and how high you're going to climb. For every 3 miles, allow around 1 hour.

For every 330 feet of height you will climb along the way, add an extra 10 minutes.

For example, if you're walking 6 miles along a path that climbs 650 feet, it will take you around 2 hours and 20 minutes to complete your trip.

If you're hiking or cycling, make sure you plan your route well—and always check the weather forecast.

WHAT IS... YODELING?

YO-DE-LAY-HEE-HO! Can you hear that strange noise echoing through the valleys? This way of singing has been used in the Alps for hundreds of years. To yodel, you need to constantly swap between singing in a very high voice and a very low voice, making a long—and loud!—wavering sound. When it's done properly, the noise can travel a long way, particularly in a place like this. Before telephones existed, people living in the Alps used yodeling to call from one village to another, or from mountain to mountain.

Avoid walking on slopes covered in scree (loose stones). You can easily lose your footing. Watch out for cliff edges and ravines, too.

HOW TO... MAKE YOUR OWN TRAIL MIX

When you spend a long time outdoors, it's important to take regular breaks and eat and drink the right things. This trail mix recipe is perfect for keeping your energy levels up:

1 big handful of nuts (try peanuts, cashews, or pecans)

1 small handful of chocolate chips

1 small handful of dried fruit (raisins, apricots, and banana chips all work well)

Always make sure you have enough daylight to get back. If you get benighted (stuck in darkness) on a mountain, it can be difficult and dangerous to find your way back.

WAYS TO HELP THE ALPS

LEAVE NO TRACE

Always make sure you never leave anything behind. Take all your litter with you, even fruit peels and apple cores. Banana skins can take two years to decompose!

KEEP STREAMS CLEAN

If you need to go to the bathroom, try to make sure you don't go near running water.

YOUR ESSENTIAL MOUNTAIN ADVENTURE KIT LIST

Heading into the hills? This is what to pack:

Water

Food

Whistle

Compass

Headlamp (with batteries)

Waterproof jacket

Warm top

Gloves

Hat

Sunglasses

Sunscreen

Basic first aid kit

Map

A fully charged phone

ARABIAN DESERT

The temperature is scorching. The wind feels like a blast of air from an oven. You're in the Arabian Desert, a baking-hot expanse where the days are long, sweaty, and exhausting. Not a single cloud floats above the dunes, and wherever you turn you see sand, sand, and more sand. But although the desert might seem empty and bone-dry, if you look closely, you'll find plants, birds, animals—and even water. Anyone who lives or travels here has to learn an important lesson: that exploring this environment needs time, determination, and patience.

FACT FILE

» The Arabian Desert is the second-largest desert on the planet, covering about 8.8 million square miles—an area roughly two and a half times the size of the US.

» The temperature in summer sometimes rises above 122 °F, making it one of the hottest places on the planet.

» The Arabian Desert is more than just sand dunes. You'll also find hills, valleys, rocks, and even a few lush areas of greenery. A fertile area like this is called an oasis.

» The desert covers parts of eight different countries: Saudi Arabia, Yemen, Oman, the United Arab Emirates, Qatar, Kuwait, Iraq, and Jordan.

THINGS TO REMEMBER

The days are hot, but the nights can get very cold.

Water and shade can save your life.

Walking on soft sand is difficult and tiring.

The desert heat is very dry, with almost zero humidity.

WHO **LIVES** HERE?

Humans have lived here for many thousands of years, finding ways to survive in the heat. Traditionally, many of the peoples who lived in the desert were nomads, which means they moved from area to area every few months, rather than having one fixed home. The most famous of these peoples are the Bedouin, who learned long ago how to breed camels and sheep, and who carry large tents with them on their travels. Some Bedouin groups still live a nomadic lifestyle today. The desert is so big that towns and even cities have been built here too, though most of the region is still wilderness.

WHAT ELSE **SURVIVES** HERE?

Mammals, birds, and reptiles are all found here in the Arabian Desert—but they can be difficult to spot. Desert animals have had to adapt to survive in the extreme environment.

Arabian oryxes have white coats that reflect the desert sunlight.

Horned desert vipers stay camouflaged thanks to their speckled, sand-colored scales.

Sand cats spend the daytime in burrows to avoid the fierce heat, then hunt at night.

WHY ARE **CAMELS SO WELL SUITED TO THE DESERT?**

For more than 3,000 years people here have used Arabian camels to help them travel around. This species of camel has one hump and is also known as a dromedary. The animals are so good at surviving here that they're known as "ships of the desert." But what makes them so special?

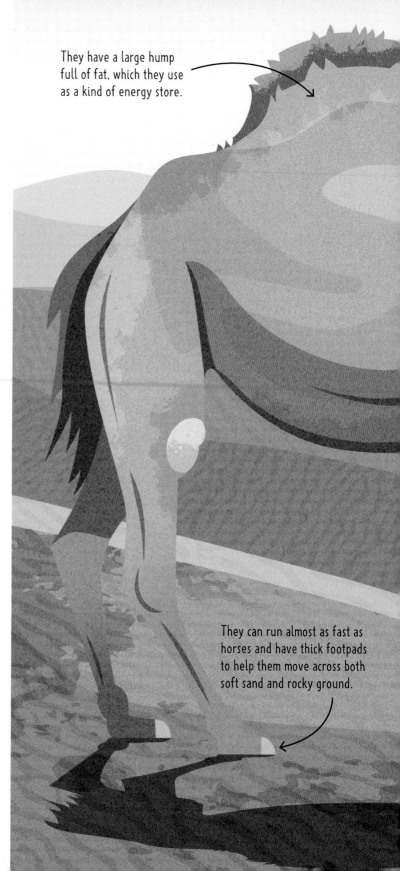

They have a large hump full of fat, which they use as a kind of energy store.

They can run almost as fast as horses and have thick footpads to help them move across both soft sand and rocky ground.

Their sharp teeth and strong lips mean they can feed on thorny desert plants.

They have three eyelids on each eye, and long eyelashes to stop sand from getting in their eyes. They can even close their nostrils too!

Camels can go for weeks at a time without a drink of water. We humans can only last two or three days!

OTHER DESERTS

A desert is somewhere with very little rainfall and very few plants. It's usually sandy or rocky. There are some amazing desert landscapes around the world.

In the US, the Mojave Desert is the driest place in North America. Snakes, hawks, and lizards all live here. The hottest part of the whole desert is an area known as Death Valley.

In Asia, the Gobi Desert is a rain shadow, which means the mountains at its edge block any rain from falling there. "Gobi" means "waterless place" in Mongolian.

Stretching right across North Africa, the Sahara is the world's largest desert. Its wildlife is incredibly varied, from slow-moving desert snails to fast-running Saharan cheetahs.

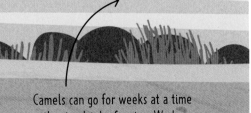

WHAT TO DO...
IN A SANDSTORM

It hardly ever rains in the desert—but that doesn't mean there aren't storms. Sandstorms happen when strong, violent winds whip up clouds of sand, turning the air thick with swirling dust. They're not common, but they can be dangerous.

If you're unlucky enough to be in the middle of one, it's important to stop sand getting into your nose, mouth, and eyes. Use a mask and goggles if you have them. If not, cover your face with a piece of clothing. If you can, find a boulder or wall to crouch behind until the storm passes.

In 1994, an Italian man running a marathon across the Sahara Desert got caught in a sandstorm and lost his way completely. He survived for nine days by sheltering in an empty building and eating bats and reptiles!

WHAT IS...
THE EMPTY QUARTER?

The Empty Quarter, or Rub' al-Khali in Arabic, is an enormous area of sand dunes in the south of the Arabian Desert. It measures about 810 miles from end to end. The punishing heat and harsh conditions here have made it famous among explorers and adventurers. In the early 1930s, with the help of local guides, an Englishman named Bertram Thomas set out to cross the Empty Quarter. It took him 59 days.

The Empty Quarter

If you're in a vehicle, make sure the driver lets some air out of the tires before driving on soft sand. Fully inflated tires get stuck very easily!

THREE WAYS TO... **LOOK FOR WATER**

Staying hydrated is crucial to surviving in the desert, so carrying water with you is extremely important. But what do you do if you run out? Here are some tips for finding water.

Rocks and boulders can provide shade... but scorpions like shade too! Poke around gently with a stick to make sure it's safe before you shelter.

1 Follow signs of life. Birds, desert animals, bees, and mosquitoes are all drawn to water. If you see birds circling in the air, there's a good chance water is nearby.

2 Look for desert trails. By following tracks made by someone else, you might find your way to water, or at least to other people.

Save your energy by walking at night rather than in the heat of the day. Walking when it's hot means you lose a lot of important body fluid through sweat.

3 Dig underground. When rain falls, it can pool and trickle into the sand and soil. Try digging deep into the ground at the base of hard rocky slopes, or into the lowest point of a dry riverbed.

Don't throw anything away. This is good advice anywhere, but here in the desert an empty tin can could be used as a cup, a cooking pot, or even a shovel.

? **WAYS TO HELP** DESERTS

THINK ABOUT THE LAND

Deserts can be affected by everything from air pollution and war damage to climate change. Even small long-term temperature changes can impact desert plants and animals.

DRIVE WITH CARE

If you're traveling in a four-wheel-drive vehicle, it's very important that it doesn't damage the desert habitat.

PROTECT OTHER PLACES

Our deserts are magical—but we don't need more of them. Some hot places are at risk of becoming deserts, as trees are cut down and the soil becomes drier.

AFRICAN **SAVANNAH**

Standing on the green, rolling grasslands of the African savannah, you're surrounded by life. Lions prowl, antelopes graze, and elephants plod across the plains. The skies are full of chattering birds and the rivers ripple with hefty hippos and lurking crocodiles. It's an awesome part of the world, where towering giraffes chew leaves from the trees and orange sunsets melt over the horizon. The wild animals and wide landscapes make this a wonderful place to be, but there are many dangers to watch out for too.

FACT FILE

» The word "savannah" describes tropical grasslands where the temperatures are warm all year. Many different African countries have areas of savannah.

» African savannahs usually have heavy monsoon rains in the summer and stay dry in the winter.

» The most famous areas of African savannah include the Serengeti in Tanzania and the Maasai Mara in Kenya.

THINGS TO **REMEMBER**

Many of the wild animals here are dangerous (and some are VERY big!).

Because it's hot and there aren't many trees, finding shelter from the sun can be hard.

If you're here in the wet season, the rain can be very heavy.

It's very warm in the day, but often gets cold at night.

WHO **LIVES** HERE?

Humans have lived in the savannah for a very long time. Traditionally, many of them are herders—people who graze sheep and cattle. Peoples like the Maasai were originally "semi-nomadic," which means they moved from place to place around the savannah, depending on the season. Many still live in small villages. Since non-Indigenous people arrived in the savannah in the last 200 years, many Maasai people have been unfairly forced to leave their homes and land, meaning they have had to find new ways of living and supporting themselves.

The traditional Maasai dress is a thick cloth called a Shuka, which is often bright red.

WHAT ELSE **SURVIVES** HERE?

Every bird and animal on the African savannah is adapted to life here.

Cheetahs have very flexible backbones to help them run fast.

Elephants use their long trunks to tear off leaves and branches to eat.

Rhinos let oxpecker birds sit on their backs to eat the insects that live on their skin.

HOW TO . . .
CALCULATE THE SUNSET

Many animals are at their most active at the end of the day, so it's always useful to know how long it is until sunset. Here's a trick for figuring it out.

First, put your sunglasses on. Then, while facing the afternoon sun (but taking care not to look directly into it!) stretch your arm in front of you. Turn your wrist so your palm is facing you, then hold your four fingers just above the horizon. Each finger means 15 minutes until sunset, so four fingers is an hour. Keep moving up, hand on top of hand, counting in hours and minutes until you reach the sun.

WHAT TO DO IF...
A LION CHARGES AT YOU

Lions are clever, majestic animals, but they can also be scary! They very rarely charge at humans. If a lion does charge you, it's probably because it feels threatened. It will usually be a mock—or pretend—charge.

The first rule is: don't run away. The lion is more than fast enough to catch you.

Don't turn your back, either. Instead, try to stand tall, wave your arms around, make lots of noise, and slowly back away. When the lion sees that you're backing away, it will usually back away itself.

WHAT IS... AFRICA'S GREAT MIGRATION?

Every year, more than two million wildebeest, gazelles, and zebras travel long distances across the savannahs of East Africa. They're following the rains in search of food, moving to places where the grass is greener. Sometimes they have to cross crocodile-infested rivers, which is very risky.

WAYS TO HELP THE SAVANNAH

HELP END POACHING

Tragically, some African animals are still hunted and killed—but charities like Save the Rhino and Save the Elephants work tirelessly to stop poachers.

BUY SOMEONE A SPECIAL PRESENT

The Maasai people traditionally make beautiful beadwork and blankets. You can help to support them by buying these things.

PLAN A DREAM SAFARI

The money from responsible safari tourism helps protect the savannah and its animals.

THE HIMALAYAS

You're standing on the rocky, icy slopes of the Himalayas, home to the highest mountains in the world. Giant snow-capped peaks spear up into the blue sky. Nowhere on Earth is further above the sea or closer to space. Eagles soar above the glaciers, shaggy yaks roam the valleys, and strings of rainbow-colored prayer flags flutter in the chilly wind. It's remote, wild, and often very, very cold, with long winters and short summers. The beauty of the mountains is unforgettable, but life can be difficult for the people who live here.

THINGS TO REMEMBER

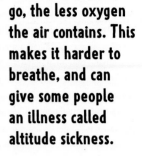

The higher up you go, the less oxygen the air contains. This makes it harder to breathe, and can give some people an illness called altitude sickness.

The weather can be extreme: as well as snow and ice, there are strong winds and bright sunshine. You need to keep warm and protect your eyes and skin from the sun.

The people who live here know about the dangers of the mountains, so always listen to their advice.

FACT FILE

» The Himalayas is a huge mountain range stretching over five Asian countries: Nepal, Bhutan, India, Pakistan, and China.

» Mountaineers and hikers from around the world love coming here for outdoor adventures.

» The highest point in the Himalayas (and the world!) is Mount Everest, which stands 29,032 feet tall.

WHO LIVES HERE?

The tallest peaks in the Himalayas are too high to live on, but people do live in villages in the valleys lower down. Because they spend their lives here, their bodies are used to the low oxygen levels in the air. Some keep animals such as yaks and goats, and often wear thick clothes made from their wool. Many Himalayan people are Buddhists, so it's common to see religious shrines and prayer flags. The local Sherpa people are well-known as skilled mountain climbers and guides. One of them, a man named Tenzing Norgay, was one of the first two people to reach the top of Mount Everest, in 1953.

WHAT ELSE SURVIVES HERE?

To survive here, plants and animals have to be tough. Not many creatures can live at such a high altitude.

Snow leopards have thick coats and wide furry paws to help them walk over ice and snow.

Himalayan jumping spiders survive by eating smaller insects blown up the mountains by the wind.

Bar-headed geese have large lungs to help them breathe as they fly over the mountains.

HOW TO... STAY WARM IN THE MOUNTAINS

The Himalayas can be fiercely cold. The best way to stay warm is to wear the right clothes.

Wear lots of layers. It's better to wear lots of thin layers than one bulky coat, because each layer helps to trap your body heat.

Have a good warm hat that covers your ears, and cozy gloves. Some people wear an inner pair and a bigger outer pair.

At high altitude, the mountain air is very cold and dry. If you wear a thin neck-warmer over your mouth when you're hiking, the air you breathe will be warmer and moister.

Sunlight reflects off snow, so wear snow goggles or sunglasses to protect your eyes from the glare.

Keep your feet as warm as possible, with thick socks and strong boots.

HOW TO... AVOID ALTITUDE SICKNESS

Most humans live fairly close to sea level, so our bodies need time to adjust to being thousands of miles higher than usual. The best way to do this—and to stop yourself getting headaches and altitude sickness—is to take things slowly.

- When you arrive in the mountains, take two or three days to rest. Drink plenty of water. Don't rush anything.

- If you're heading even higher, don't climb too far in one day. Let your body get used to each new altitude. Himalayan climbers often use the motto "climb high, sleep low," which means they always return to a lower altitude to spend the night.

- If you don't feel well, move back down the mountains.

WHAT TO DO... IF YOU GET CAUGHT IN AN AVALANCHE

An avalanche happens when a huge mass of snow slides down the mountain. They can be very big and powerful. If you can't get out of the way, this is the best way to survive.

- Use your arms and legs to "swim" with the snow, trying to stay close to the surface.
- Don't shout or scream—you might get a mouthful of snow.
- If you're buried under snow when the avalanche stops, quickly bring your arms to your face and dig out a space to breathe.
- The avalanche might have turned you upside-down, so spit to see which way is up. Your spit will always fall straight down. Try to dig your way out, heading straight up.

If you're camping, don't pitch your tent anywhere that might flood or be hit by an avalanche or rockfall.

OTHER MOUNTAIN RANGES

Our planet has many mighty mountain ranges, each with its own wildlife.

In the Andes in South America, enormous condors fly high above the mountain ridges, and llamas and alpacas graze in the valleys.

In the Caucasus Mountains, where Europe meets Asia, blue gentians, pink primulas, and other colorful wildflowers pattern the slopes.

In the Sierra Nevadas in the US, mountain lions slink through the forests and bighorn sheep scale the steep slopes.

WAYS TO HELP THE HIMALAYAS

AVOID CROWDED MOUNTAINS

Sometimes so many people want to climb the same mountain that the slopes become too busy. If you can, try to choose quieter mountain trails.

USE A GUIDE

Many local Sherpa people work as expert mountain guides. By hiring a guide, you'll not only stay safe, but also learn how to look after the mountain as you explore.

LEAVE NOTHING BEHIND

In 2019, a horrifying 12 tons of trash was cleared from Mount Everest. Wherever you go, never leave anything behind.

AUSTRALIAN OUTBACK

The earth is red and scorched. The horizon wobbles with heat. The sun beats down on a silent, almost cloudless land, a place where reptiles slither and kangaroos scratch around for food. You're in the outback—the dry, dusty center of the enormous country of Australia, far from the crashing waves, busy cities, and green forests of the coast. The outback is an extreme environment to be in—but people have lived here for tens of thousands of years.

FACT FILE

» Most of the outback is arid or semi-arid, which means it's very dry and gets little rainfall. In many places, a few skinny acacia trees provide the only shade.

» Although a lot of it looks like a desert, it also has rivers and mountainous areas.

» Other names for the outback include "the bush" and "the never-never."

» Uluru is an enormous, world-famous rock in the middle of the outback. It stands alone, rising out of the surrounding plains, at 1,141 feet tall. It is a very important sacred site for the Anangu people who live nearby.

THINGS TO REMEMBER

 It gets incredibly hot here, and there's not much shade.

 The distances between towns and villages in the outback are huge.

 Finding water can be very difficult.

 It's a dramatic and beautiful landscape, but it can be deadly.

WHO **LIVES** HERE?

Aboriginal people have lived in the Australian outback for thousands of years. Many of them have a very close, spiritual connection to the land. Some still use traditional skills to predict the local weather, find food in the wilderness, and read marks on the ground to see which animals have passed by.

More than 200 years ago, non-Indigenous people began arriving in Australia from other countries. Some stole land from the Aboriginal people and treated them very badly. Since then, it has been recognized how wrong these actions were. Today, people from many different backgrounds live in the outback.

WHAT ELSE **SURVIVES** HERE?

It often looks empty, but plenty of animals have adapted to survive in the outback, from tiny spiders to feathery emus.

Dingoes are large wild dogs with sharp teeth for catching prey, and short fur to help them stay cool.

Red kangaroos move quickly without getting too tired by bouncing across the land.

Saltwater crocodiles live at the very northern edge of the outback. They have powerful tails for swimming in creeks and rivers.

FOOD IN THE OUTBACK

Over thousands of years, Aboriginal people have learned that if you search hard, the sun-baked land of the outback holds many different foods. These include:

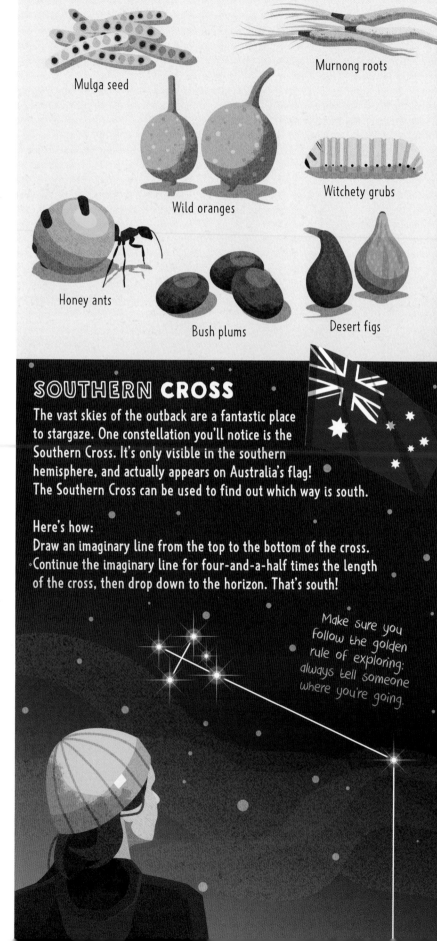

Mulga seed

Murnong roots

Wild oranges

Witchety grubs

Honey ants

Bush plums

Desert figs

SOUTHERN **CROSS**

The vast skies of the outback are a fantastic place to stargaze. One constellation you'll notice is the Southern Cross. It's only visible in the southern hemisphere, and actually appears on Australia's flag! The Southern Cross can be used to find out which way is south.

Here's how:
Draw an imaginary line from the top to the bottom of the cross. Continue the imaginary line for four-and-a-half times the length of the cross, then drop down to the horizon. That's south!

Make sure you follow the golden rule of exploring: always tell someone where you're going.

HOW TO... **THROW A BOOMERANG**

A boomerang is a curved piece of wood traditionally used by Aboriginal people as a weapon for hunting.

Use your thumb and fingers to hold it at the bottom of one end, with the bend in the boomerang pointing behind you. Don't aim too high—try aiming for the treetops in the distance. Tilt the boomerang away from you slightly, then flick your arm forward to release it. You don't need to throw it hard. Have fun practicing!

HOW TO... **RECOGNIZE ANIMAL TRACKS**

Each type of animal leaves its own pattern of tracks in the dusty ground of the outback.

If you have to run away from a crocodile (which is VERY unlikely!), sprint as fast as you can in a straight line. Crocs can run, but most humans can run faster—and further!

Snake

Kangaroo

Emu

Dingo

WAYS TO **HELP** THE AUSTRALIAN OUTBACK

FIGHT CLIMATE CHANGE

In a place this hot and dry, even a slight rise in temperatures can have a devastating effect on the plants, animals, and people who live here.

LEARN ABOUT INDIGENOUS CULTURE

Aboriginal people have lived in the outback for thousands of years. Their way of life teaches everyone to protect and respect the land.

DON'T WASTE WATER

Drinking is very important in the heat of the outback—but remember that water is precious here.

ANTARCTICA

Welcome to the empty continent. All around you, stretching into the distance, is a vast white wilderness. Your breath turns to clouds in the still icy air, and frost is forming on your eyelashes. Only a lucky few people ever come here, and the rest of the world feels far, far away. On the coast there are pale mountains, wide bays, and shimmering icebergs, but inland you could hike for weeks and find nothing but frozen horizons and an endless polar silence. Here in Antarctica, perhaps more than anywhere, you need to think extra-carefully about everything you do.

⚠ THINGS TO **REMEMBER**

Because the air is so dry, you'll get thirsty very easily.

In winter, even the surrounding ocean freezes over.

When it's windy, it can be strong enough to blow over a small vehicle.

Even in summer, the temperatures in most parts of Antarctica are below freezing.

FACT FILE

» Antarctica is the coldest continent in the world, and the fifth largest, covering nearly as much land as the whole of South America.

» No one owns Antarctica, but several countries have research bases here, including Argentina, China, Germany, Russia, the UK, and the US.

» It's almost completely covered by a sheet of ice averaging 1¼ miles thick. In fact, about 90% of all the world's ice is here in Antarctica.

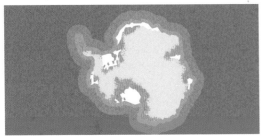

Antarctica from above

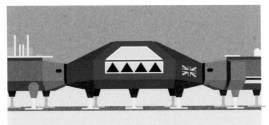

Halley VI Research Station

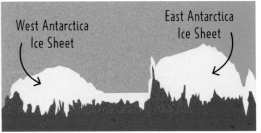

West Antarctica Ice Sheet

East Antarctica Ice Sheet

Cross-section through Antarctica

WHO **LIVES** HERE?

The short answer is: almost nobody! Because it's so cold, Antarctica doesn't have a permanent population like other continents. You won't find any villages or towns. However, there are always a few thousand scientists and researchers here. They live and work in specially designed research bases, which have been built to survive extremely low temperatures. People usually stay for a few weeks or months at a time, studying things like Antarctic wildlife, pollution, or the changing climate. The continent's vast frozen emptiness also makes it an incredible adventure for explorers.

WHAT ELSE **SURVIVES** HERE?

The middle of Antarctica is a difficult place for anything to survive, but some unusual creatures live near the coastline.

Weddell seals can dive deep under the sea ice to find fish.

Emperor penguins huddle together in groups to stay warm in the cold.

Snow petrels have white feathers to blend in with the snow and ice.

Icefish are so well adapted to the cold that their blood is cloudy white!

HOW TO ... **LOOK AFTER THE PEOPLE YOU'RE WITH**

If you're on an adventure in Antarctica, one of the main risks is hypothermia, when your body loses heat too fast. It can be very dangerous.

Covering your whole body with extra-warm layers is the best way to stay warm enough—but it's also very important to look after the people you're with.

If you spot a white patch of frozen skin on someone's face, this is a danger sign. And look out for what people call "the umbles," which is when someone starts mumbling, stumbling, fumbling, or grumbling!

All of these could be signs of hypothermia. Help the person by getting them warmer right away, keeping them dry, and giving them warm drinks.

Staying active will help you stay warm. Sit-ups, jumping jacks, and push-ups are all good!

Be very careful on sea ice. It can crack, break up, and float away—with you standing on it!

WHAT WAS... THE RACE TO THE SOUTH POLE?

The South Pole is the point at the very bottom of the world map. It sits in the middle of the Antarctic wilderness, hundreds of miles from the nearest coastline, across freezing icy plains.

In 1911, two explorers tried to become the first to get to the South Pole: a Norwegian named Roald Amundsen, and a British explorer, Robert Falcon Scott. Both had teams of other people with them, as well as dogs, tents, and supplies.

After struggling across the ice for many hard weeks, Amundsen's team reached the South Pole on December 14, 1911. Scott and his team didn't arrive until a month later, on January 17, 1912. It was only when Scott saw Amundsen's flag planted into the ice that he knew he'd lost the race. The bravery of both men has gone down in history.

Sometimes so much snow is blowing around that you can't even see your hand in front of your face. This is called a whiteout. Some explorers train for whiteouts by putting white buckets over their heads and trying to move around!

WHAT SHOULD YOU EAT AND DRINK ON AN EXPEDITION?

Very few plants grow here, so finding food in the wild is virtually impossible. This means that you need to bring what you're going to eat. Choose things that are simple to pack, easy to heat, and won't rot—frozen, dried, and canned foods are all good.

Fatty foods will give you warmth and energy. Some people here eat eight chocolate bars a day—they might not be good for your teeth, but they contain lots of calories which will give you energy to keep you warm.

Having lots to drink is very important too. The good news is that most of the ice here can be melted into drinking water!

⚠ WAYS TO HELP ANTARCTICA

THINK ABOUT POLLUTION

Pollution from other continents affects Antarctica. By making green choices at home, you're helping here too!

SUPPORT ENVIRONMENTAL ACTION

Groups like the Antarctic and Southern Ocean Coalition do vital work to protect the area.

LOOK AFTER THE ECOSYSTEM

If you're lucky enough to come here, never bring any non-native plants, seeds, or animals with you.

OUTER SPACE

Let's go into the great beyond. High above the seas, high above the mountains, up and up until Earth becomes a distant blue and green ball. Out here, there is no wildlife, no noise, and almost no gravity. A trip into space is the ultimate adventure, but it's one that only a tiny number of people ever experience. Can you imagine what it must be like to drift through the deep black universe so far away from home? It takes a lot of hard work and many years of training to become an astronaut—but the rewards are incredible.

FACT FILE

» Where does the sky end and space begin? Some experts say it's at a boundary known as the Kármán Line, 62 miles above Earth's surface. To give you an idea of how high this is, most airplanes never get more than 7 miles off the ground!

» Earth is one of eight planets orbiting the sun. The others are Mercury, Venus, Mars, Jupiter, Saturn, Uranus, and Neptune. They all form part of our solar system, which is just one small area of the Milky Way galaxy.

» The solar system also contains almost 200 moons (including our own!), dwarf planets like Pluto, and millions of asteroids, meteoroids, and comets.

WHAT'S IT LIKE ON THE **INTERNATIONAL SPACE STATION?**

The International Space Station, or ISS, is the largest space station ever built. End to end, it's the length of a full-size football field! The ISS has been in space since 1998, traveling around the world at a height of 250 miles. It makes a full circuit of the planet every 90 minutes, going all the way around the world 16 times a day.

It has a crew of six astronauts, with specially trained men and women from different countries taking turns to live and work there. They usually spend around six months on the station. The astronauts feel weightless when they're on board, which means they can float from room to room.

The ISS has six bedrooms, two bathrooms, and a gym. Being in space can make astronauts' muscles smaller, since they are not using them to work against gravity—so they have to spend at least two hours a day exercising. They sleep in special sleeping bags attached to the walls.

Whenever a spacecraft visits the ISS, it brings food and supplies. The astronauts drink through straws from enclosed containers. They have three meals a day, eating things like peanut butter, fruit, nuts, chicken, seafood, and brownies. But they can't use normal salt and pepper with their food, because it would float off everywhere!

WHAT DO **ASTRONAUTS WEAR ON SPACEWALKS?**

Sometimes astronauts need to go outside the space station to test equipment or do experiments. This is called a spacewalk. It usually lasts between five and eight hours. To stay safe, astronauts are attached to the space station by a tether, or rope.

To survive in the vacuum of empty space, each astronaut wears a spacesuit, which has its own supply of oxygen to breathe and water to drink. The suits have to protect the astronauts in extreme conditions—the temperature in space can be as hot as 248 °F and as cold as -238 °F! Spacesuit gloves even have little heaters in the fingertips. Inside the helmet, earphones and a microphone let the astronauts talk to the rest of the crew. Some astronauts wear backpacks with thruster jets, which means they can fly back to the station if their tether gets detached.

Staying clean can be tricky in space. Astronauts use liquid soap and special shampoo that doesn't need to be rinsed. When their clothes get dirty, they can't wash them, so they have to take enough underwear for the whole trip!

WHAT ARE...
ASTEROIDS, METEOROIDS, AND COMETS?

Asteroids, meteoroids, and comets all fly through space, orbiting the sun. But how are they different?

A comet is a mass of ice and dust. This ice and dust sometimes forms a long "tail" behind the comet.

An asteroid is a big lump of space rock. Some asteroids are almost 600 miles wide!

Humans have made nine missions to the Moon, including the first landing in 1969. It takes around three days to fly there from Earth in a spaceship. The moon is almost 1,000 times further away from us than the International Space Station.

A meteoroid is a much smaller piece of stone or metal, which has broken off from an asteroid. Some are the size of pebbles.

If a space rock enters Earth's atmosphere, it creates a streak of light called a meteor. This is what some people call a shooting star.

If a space rock lands on the surface of a planet or moon, it is called a meteorite.

⚠ WAYS TO HELP SPACE

KEEP IT CLEAN
When astronauts visit the moon, or any other place in space, they have to take care not to bring any harmful germs or contamination from Earth.

USE GREEN TECHNOLOGY
It takes a lot of fuel to reach space, so scientists are trying to develop more eco-friendly ways to power spacecrafts.

LEARN NEW FACTS
Organizations like the National Aeronautics and Space Administration (which is known as NASA) and the European Space Agency (ESA) often share their latest discoveries online.

THE FUTURE

As humans, many of our survival skills have stayed the same for thousands of years. But what about the future? As the world's population grows and the planet changes, will we need to find new ways of staying safe and healthy?

INSECTS FOR LUNCH

Farmers need lots of space to graze animals like cows and sheep, and to grow food for the animals to feed on. This means humans will probably have to eat less meat in the future. Some scientists think more and more people will farm insects instead! Ants, termites, beetles, and silkworms are already eaten in some countries. They contain lots of protein, which the human body needs.

FLOATING CITIES

If sea levels continue to rise, there might be a time when some towns and cities are impossible to live in. One solution could be building cities that float. Experts have designed special sea platforms that would link together and make cities big enough for 10,000 people, without killing the marine life below. Can you imagine living in the middle of the sea?

UNDERGROUND FARMS

In many parts of the world it can be hard for people to find enough outdoor space to farm plants and vegetables. One answer is to grow crops underground, in old tunnels, cellars, or shelters. There are already underground farms in countries like the UK and France. They use clever technology and artificial lights instead of soil and sunlight.

SOLAR-PANELED HATS

Imagine hiking through the desert using an electronic device to guide you. What would you do when the battery ran out? With a solar-paneled hat, you wouldn't just be sheltered from the sun, you'd also be able to plug your device into your hat to charge it. Solar-paneled hats and backpacks—and even solar-powered cars—have all been invented.

EDIBLE CUTLERY

We all know that plastic cutlery and food packaging can be bad for the planet. But what if your cutlery and packaging could be eaten after you use it? Inventions already include drink cartons made from seaweed, bowls made from wheat, and cutlery made from flour.

LIVING ON MARS

Scientists think that one day we might be able to go and live on other planets—though it would be very complicated and expensive to build shelters where people could survive. They say that Mars is the planet that would be best suited to human life, because it has sunlight and seasons, and its days are around 24 hours long. On the downside, it's much colder than Earth, has almost no water, and it could take nine months to get there!

THE FUTURE IS YOURS

As humans, we have the skills and intelligence to shape the world around us into a better place. That includes you!

Young people like you have started campaigns and movements that have completely changed the way we look at things. If you have an idea that could make a difference, shout it from the rooftops!

Maybe you'll help develop an exciting new technology, or use your creativity to protect the natural world. You might train to be an underwater scientist, a wildlife conservationist, or even a robotics engineer. Who knows—your future job might not even be invented yet!

GLOSSARY

CAMOUFLAGE To hide from danger by using the same colors or patterns as your environment to disguise yourself. Some animals have natural markings or colors to allow them to do this, but humans can also do this with their clothes or by painting their skin.

CAMPAIGN To organize activities and events to try to bring about change.

COMMUNITY A group of people living in a specific area or who share the same interests, history, or culture.

CLIMATE CHANGE Changes in Earth's weather patterns caused by **global warming**, such as hotter days, more rainfall, and stronger storms.

DECOMPOSE To break down into smaller parts naturally after death (referring to plants and animals).

DEFORESTATION Cutting down trees in a large area, leading to the destruction of forests.

EMISSIONS Gases, such as carbon dioxide, that are created by human activity and released into the air.

GLOBAL WARMING An increase in Earth's temperature, caused by larger amounts of gases like carbon dioxide collecting in the air around Earth.

HUMIDITY A measure of how much water there is in the air.

HYDRATED When you have drunk enough water or other liquid to allow your body to work properly.

INDIGENOUS PEOPLE Groups of people who are descended from the first people to live in a place, rather than people from other places and cultures who later made their homes there. Also sometimes known as First Peoples.

POACHER Someone who hunts and catches or kills wild animals without permission, usually to make money from selling the animals or parts of the animals.

SACRED Special or holy for people who are part of a particular religion or culture.

SETTLEMENTS Places where groups of people decide to make their homes together, such as villages or towns.